GREETINGS from PANAMA CITY FLA.

Greetings from PANAMA CITY FLA.

GREETINGS from PANAMA CITY FLA.

Greetings from PANAMA CITY FLA.

GREETINGS from PANAMA CITY FLA.

Greetings from PANAMA CITY FLA.

GREETINGS from PANAMA CITY FLA.

Greetings from PANAMA CITY FLA.

GREETINGS from PANAMA CITY FLA.

Greetings from PANAMA CITY FLA.

Greetings from PANAMA CITY FLA.

Greetings from PANAMA CITY FLA.

GREETINGS from PANAMA CITY FLA.

Printed in the USA
CPSIA information can be obtained
at www.ICGtesting.com
LVHW040513170324
774645LV00004B/567

9 798385 407941